How Did That Get Here?

The Biography of Bananas

Rachel Eagen

Crabtree Publishing Company

www.crabtreebooks.com

Crabtree Publishing Company
www.crabtreebooks.com

For Rachelle: you're okay, kid.

Coordinating editor: Ellen Rodger
Series editor: Carrie Gleason
Editors: Adrianna Morganelli, L. Michelle Nielsen
Design and production coordinator: Rosie Gowsell
Cover design and production assistance: Samara Parent
Art direction: Rob MacGregor
Scanning technician: Arlene Arch-Wilson
Photo research: Allison Napier

Photo Credits:
AP/Wide World Photos: p. 9 (bottom), p. 11 (bottom), p. 26, p. 28; The Art Archive/National Archives Washington DC: p. 17; Gary Braasch /Corbis: p. 21 (bottom), p. 23 (top); Vo Trung Dung/Corbis Sygma: p. 27, p. 30 (bottom); Owen Franken/Corbis: p. 1, p. 24; Louise Gubb/Corbis Saba: cover; Earl & Nazima Kowall/Corbis: p. 9 (top); Lake County Museum/Corbis: p. 21 (top); The Mariners' Museum/Corbis: p. 16, p. 19; Christine Osborne/Corbis: p. 7; Pablo Corral V/Corbis: p. 20, p. 25 (bottom); Oswaldo Rivas/Reuters/Corbis: p. 29; Swim Ink 2, LLC/Corbis: p. 4; Underwood & Underwood/Corbis: p. 18; Orlando Sierra/AFP/Getty Images: p. 10; Josef Polleross/The Image Works: p. 22; Sean Sprague/The Image Works: p. 5 (top); Jean-Yves Bendeyt/istock International: p. 5 (left); Suzannah Skelton/istock International: p. 13 (top left); Leigh Wood/istock International: p. 8; Maximilian Stock LTD/maXximages.com: p. 13 (middle right); North Wind Picture

Archives: p. 15; Philip Wolmuth/Panos Pictures: p. 31; Food Collection/Superstock: p. 13 (middle left). Other images from stock cd.

Cartography: Jim Chernishenko: p. 6

Cover: A girl in Uganda, in eastern Africa, carries bananas to market.

Title page: Bananas and their close relative, plantains, are eaten frequently in areas where they grow.

Contents page: Bananas grow on trees in the tropics. Bananas are picked, or harvested when still green.

Crabtree Publishing Company
www.crabtreebooks.com   1-800-387-7650

Cataloging-in-Publication Data
Eagen, Rachel, 1979-
 The biography of bananas / written by Rachel Eagen.
  p. cm. -- (How did that get here?)
 ISBN-13: 978-0-7787-2483-4 (rlb)
 ISBN-10: 0-7787-2483-2 (rlb)
 ISBN-13: 978-0-7787-2519-0 (pb)
 ISBN-10: 0-7787-2519-7 (pb)
 1. Bananas--Juvenile literature. I. Title. II. Series.
 SB379.B2E24 2005
 634'.772--dc22
                                     2005019022
                                           LC

Published in the United States
PMB 16A
350 Fifth Ave.
Suite 3308
New York, NY
10118

Published in Canada
616 Welland Ave.
St. Catharines
Ontario, Canada
L2M 5V6

Published in the United Kingdom
73 Lime Walk
Headington
Oxford
OX3 7AD
United Kingdom

Published in Australia
386 Mt. Alexander Rd.
Ascot Vale (Melbourne)
VIC 3032

Contents

What are Bananas?

Bananas are the most popular fruit in the world. They are the fourth-largest food **staple** in the world, next to rice, wheat, and potatoes. Some people who live in tropical areas eat bananas at almost every meal. The delicate plant that produces bananas grows only in hot **tropical** climates. To get to supermarkets in North America, bananas are **exported** in large refrigerated ships called reefers. Bananas are a commodity, or a good that can be bought or sold.

The World's Largest Herb

The botanical, or scientific, name for bananas is *Musa sapientum*. Banana plants are the world's largest herbs. The stalk of the plant is made from several long, green leaves, or sheaths, which wrap around each other as they grow. Banana plants grow from 15 to 30 feet (5 to 10 meters) tall. Banana plants are endangered because they cannot fight off diseases on their own. Farmers and scientists worry that a **pandemic** of disease will wipe out the global banana crop.

An advertising poster from the 1950s showing a made-up scene of banana growing.

4

Dessert Bananas

There are over 500 different **varieties** of bananas in the world. The most popular banana in North America and Europe is the dessert banana, which is also called the Cavendish variety. Cavendish bananas have bright yellow skins and a sweet flavor. Cavendish bananas are grown on large, American-owned farms in Central America and the Caribbean. These farms, called plantations, occupy huge areas of land where thousands of people work. More than half a billion people in the world depend on the banana trade for their livelihood.

A girl in El Salvador enjoys a banana. Bananas are a healthy, hearty snack.

Fingers, Hands, and Clusters

Bananas grow in large bunches on trees. They are broken into smaller groups to sell.

▼ *Groups of four to six bananas, which are sold in supermarkets, are called clusters.*

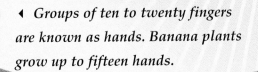

▸ *Each banana is called a finger.*

◂ *Groups of ten to twenty fingers are known as hands. Banana plants grow up to fifteen hands.*

Banana Lands

Historians believe the first **edible** bananas were found growing in the Malay Archipelago, a large group of islands in the Pacific Ocean stretching from the north of Australia to Southeast Asia. Around 1000 B.C., bananas spread to other regions of the tropics, such as the Marquesas Islands in the South Pacific, and to Hawaii. It was easy to grow bananas in the new areas because all that is needed to grow new plants are the cuttings of suckers, or baby plants, that grow around the base of mature banana plants. Traders traveling along the East Coast of Africa from Southeast Asia traded bananas and banana suckers to people along the African coast.

Producers

Approximately 28 million tons (25 million tonnes) of bananas are grown each year. Most of these are **consumed** within the countries in which they are grown. The top banana producers in the world are India, Brazil, China, Ecuador, and the Philippines. Other important banana producers include Venezuela, Honduras, and Panama. In Africa, large banana plantations are found in Cameroon, and in countries along the northwest of the continent, such as the Ivory Coast.

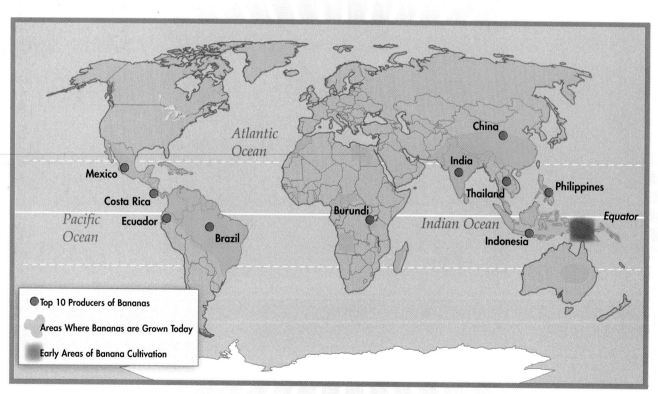

Bananas are believed to have originally grown in the Malay Archipelago. Today, banana cultivation has spread to many tropical areas.

Exporters

Only about 20 percent of the world's banana crop is exported, or sold to other countries. About 65 percent of bananas that are grown for export come from South America. The leading exporters are Colombia, Ecuador, and Costa Rica. These countries export bananas to the United States, Canada, Europe, and parts of Asia. Another 27 percent of banana exports are grown in Southeast Asia, and about seven percent of the banana crop is exported from Africa. Bananas are also grown on small farms in Florida, but they are not exported on a large scale.

Banana Farms

Bananas are grown on two types of farms. Smallholder farms are managed either by one person or a family. Most smallholder banana farms are less than five hectares (12 acres). Most of a smallholder banana farmer's crop is sold at local markets. Smallholder banana farms are found in the Caribbean, especially in the Windward Islands, an island chain including Martinique, St. Lucia, Barbados, St. Vincent, and Grenada. Plantations are large **commercial** farms, usually owned by American fruit companies. Banana plantations employ many workers and export the fruit to consumers all over the world.

A worker on a banana plantation in Oman, in the Middle East, tends the growing plants. Bananas are a major crop in Oman.

Growing Bananas

Bananas are grown in the tropics, the areas of the world just north and south of the equator. Bananas need a warm climate where rainfall is plentiful to grow and stay healthy. Cold weather prevents banana plants from producing fruit and damages the plants' leaves. Damaged banana leaves make the fruit vulnerable to sunburn. Wind is also dangerous for banana plants. Light winds can tear the fragile leaves of the plant, while strong winds can topple the plants or even destroy entire plantations.

Proper Soil

Bananas grow best in **fertile** soils that are well drained. Soils that hold water, such as clay, are unsuitable for growing bananas, because the excess water causes the roots to rot in the ground. Rocky soils and **volcanic ash** are ideal for growing bananas because they naturally allow water to seep deep into the ground and away from the roots of banana plants.

Parts of the Banana Plant

The leaves of banana plants grow up to 12 feet (four meters) long. The leaves sprout from the ground and wrap around each other very tightly, forming the stem. About two months after planting, large purplish-red buds push through the center of the stem, grow fatter, and eventually droop down to one side of the plant. Smaller purplish flowers then appear on the buds. Some of the flowers grow into bananas.

The flowers of banana plants turn into banana fruit.

Tending to the Plants

Farmers tie banana plants to long poles for support. This helps prevent the plants from falling over in heavy winds, or when they become heavy with fruit. The plants are watered, fertilized, and regularly sprayed with **fungicides** and **pesticides** to keep them free of diseases and pests. The fruit is also covered in large plastic bags to protect them from insects and birds. The bags are clear so that light can still reach the leaves, allowing the fruit to mature. Banana plants develop and produce fruit within eight to ten months of planting. This makes bananas especially suited to countries where hurricanes and other storms are frequent, because they can be grown quickly to provide food for people before the next storm hits.

Ripe and Ready

Bananas that are grown for export are picked while the fruit is still green to prevent the bananas from spoiling while they are shipped. If left on the plant, bananas develop a **pithy** texture, and the skin splits open. Bananas ripen properly and taste best if they are picked before they are fully ripe.

▸ *Bananas are grown in plastic bags.*

A banana farmer cuts weeds on a plantation in Costa Rica. Weeds are cleared from the fields so that they do not steal nutrients from the soil that banana plants need for growth.

9

New Bananas From Old

Banana plants have thick stems called rhizomes, that grow underground. Rhizomes are covered in bumps, which are similar to the eyes on potatoes. From the notches, **shoots** grow out of the ground. These new shoots are called suckers. The main banana plant is called the parent plant. The suckers are called the daughter and granddaughter plants. When banana plants are harvested, farmers cut down all but the strongest daughter and granddaughter suckers.

▶ *A young banana plant grown from a sucker of the parent plant.*

Banana Clones

Most plants produce new plants through a process called pollination, which occurs when the male part of the plant mixes with the female part of the plant. New banana plants are grown from cuttings taken from a parent plant, in a process called **vegetative propagation**. Banana plants are propagated, or reproduced from cuttings taken either from the rhizome, or from suckers. Banana plants grown from the suckers or rhizomes of the original plant are called clones, because they are exact copies of the parent plant. In the wild, banana plants pollinate themselves. Wild banana plants produce fruit that is packed with hard, bitter seeds that make the fruit inedible.

Endangered Fruit

Some scientists believe that the dessert banana will eventually be **extinct**. The suckers that sprout around the base of the parent plant contain the exact same genes, or the puzzle pieces that make a person, plant, or animal unique. All plants and animals need a mix of different genes in order to survive. Clones are often weaker copies of the original plant, because they are cultivated from the same genes over and over again. Genetic clones are **vulnerable** to insects and pests, and have difficulty fighting off diseases. Banana farmers are worried that a disease will one day wipe out the entire banana crop, and leave them nothing with which to cultivate a new crop.

(above) The Cavendish banana that is so popular in North America and Europe can be thought of as a lucky accident because it produces no pollen or seeds from which it can reproduce.

Good Sports

Even though all bananas are exactly like their parents, new types of bananas with slightly different characteristics sometimes grow unexpectedly. This happens naturally, without the help of scientists or farmers. The process is known as sporting, and the new banana varieties are called mutations. Mutations are permanent changes in genes. Mutations happen because of mistakes during **reproduction** or because of environmental factors. All banana varieties come about through sporting.

(left) The banana trees on this plantation in India are cut down to make way for new banana plants.

Types of Bananas

Today, there are over 500 types of bananas. Each banana variety grows in a specific type of soil and climate. The popular Cavendish variety, or dessert banana, makes up only about 15 percent of the bananas grown in the world each year. Most bananas are cooking bananas, and plantains, which are a starchy cousin of the banana. Cooking bananas and plantains are both part of the staple diet in the countries where they are grown.

Cavendish Comes to Town

Cavendish bananas are the most common bananas imported to North America. The yellow Cavendish banana is thought to have appeared in southern China around 1826. Until then, all bananas were either green or red. The yellow variety was discovered by Charles Telfair, a plant collector. He sent some of the banana plants to his friend in England, who eventually passed them on to the Duke of Devonshire. The Duke grew them in his greenhouse and named them after his family name, Cavendish. John Williams, a Christian missionary, brought suckers of the Cavendish variety to islands in the South Pacific, including Samoa, the Friendly Islands, and Fiji, around 1850. Within 20 years, Cavendish bananas were also being grown in the Caribbean Islands.

So Many Bananas!

◀ The Hawaiian Red banana is a popular banana in North America. It has a reddish-brown skin and yellow fruit with a creamy texture. Hawaiian Reds are also called Indio, Cuban Reds, or Morado bananas. Today, large amounts of this banana are grown in Ecuador.

▼ Finger, or Sugar, bananas are very small. They grow only to a length of about three inches (eight centimeters). They are named after their very sweet flavor.

▲ Apple bananas are slightly smaller than the Cavendish variety, and have a rectangular shape. They have a golden yellow fruit that tastes a little like apples.

▶ Plantains are used mostly for cooking. Plantains are a cousin of the banana family, are larger than the Cavendish variety, and have a bright green skin. They can be eaten on their own when they are very ripe. The pinkish fruit of a plantain is sweet when the skin has turned black.

New World Bananas

Banana cultivation spread from its place of origin to other tropical areas. By the mid-600s A.D., **Arab traders** brought banana suckers to the Middle East, where they were successfully cultivated. They also brought the fruit to the West Coast of Africa where it grew well in the hot tropical climate.

Colonies and Missionaries

In 1482, Portuguese **colonists** found bananas growing in Africa, in the present-day countries of Sierra Leone, Liberia, and Gambia.

The Portuguese took suckers from mature plants and brought them to their colonies in the Canary Islands, off the northwest coast of Africa. The Portuguese also brought bananas back to Europe, where they were sold in markets. In the 1500s, bananas came to the **New World** with European settlers. At this time, religious **missionaries** accompanied the settlers to the colonies. The missionaries, who followed a religion called **Christianity**, hoped to convert the native peoples of the New World to Christianity.

Age of Exploration

The 1400s were a time of exploration and discovery for European nations. Explorers set out to discover new lands and claim them for their kings. They discovered new plants and animals on the lands. They also introduced plants and animals from elsewhere. In the 1500s, the Spanish, French, Portuguese, Dutch, and British set up colonies in parts of Africa, North, Central, and South America, as well as on the islands of the West Indies, or present-day Caribbean. Settlers came from Europe to live in the colonies. They cultivated food crops on large farms and raised livestock. They also traded with local native peoples for jewelry and other items. Shipments of goods, such as food, spices, cotton, rum, and gold, were sent back to Europe, as well as to the colonies in Africa, where they were sold. Some colonists became very rich by selling commodities from their settlements.

The First Banana

Missionary Friar Tomas de Berlanga is believed to have been the first to bring banana plants to the New World. He brought the plants from a Portuguese settlement in the Canary Islands, to the Spanish colony of Santo Domingo, or present-day Dominican Republic. De Berlanga set up the first New World banana plantation in 1516. Banana plantations were soon established throughout European colonies in the Caribbean, as well as in South and Central America.

(background) An early banana plantation in Jamaica. Gros Michel bananas grew there until a disease wiped them out in the 1940s.

The First Banana Companies

Bananas were not known in North America until 1870. Lorenzo Dow Baker, a sea captain from Cape Cod, Massachusetts, discovered bananas when he was visiting Jamaica. Baker purchased several hands of unripe Gros Michel bananas and brought them back to Jersey City, New Jersey, where he sold them for two dollars each. This was a high price to pay for bananas but Americans liked the exotic fruit and wanted more.

The Boston Fruit Company

In 1871, Baker met a produce seller named Andrew Preston. Preston was enthusiastic about bringing bananas to America. In 1885, Baker and Preston formed the Boston Fruit Company. Preston was in charge of **overseeing** the production of bananas on plantations in the West Indies, while Baker was in charge of shipping the bananas to Boston. As the Boston Fruit Company expanded, bananas were sold in New York and Boston.

Banana Boats

Early banana businessmen had difficulties keeping bananas from rotting during the time it took to ship the fruit from the West Indies to the United States. In the early 1900s, refrigerated ships were invented that kept the bananas cool so they did not ripen as quickly. The first banana boats operating for the Boston Fruit Company were known as the "Great White Fleet." With refrigerated ships, more bananas were imported to North America. The boats also brought banana shipments to Europe.

This historic photo shows a worker at a pier unloading bananas from a conveyor belt in the United States. Bananas bruise easily so workers must take care when handling the fruit.

Minor Cooper Keith

Minor Cooper Keith was the son of a wealthy lumber merchant in Brooklyn, New York. In 1871, Keith joined his uncle and his brothers in Costa Rica to build railroads from the capital city to the coast. Around 1873, Keith planted bananas on either side of the railroad tracks to feed the workers. A business opportunity unfolded before Keith's eyes. Knowing how popular bananas had become in North America, Keith assumed that the fruit would be just as popular in South America. Keith began transporting bananas throughout Costa Rica on refrigerated rail cars. By the time the railroad was completed in 1890, it was used mostly to ship bananas throughout the country.

Keith became an important businessman in Costa Rica and soon expanded his business and exported bananas to Colombia on the railroads.

The United Fruit Company

In 1899, Keith teamed up with his competitors, Andrew Preston and Lorenzo Dow Baker. Keith controlled several banana plantations and hundreds of miles of railroads in Central America. The Boston Fruit Company controlled the banana trade in the Caribbean, and owned an enormous fleet of steamships. Together, they formed the United Fruit Company in 1899, and gained a **monopoly** over the banana trade.

Refrigerated rail cars made it possible to ship bananas long distances over land.

Cornering the Market

By the end of 1899, the banana trade was largely controlled by the United Fruit Company. Bananas had grown in popularity in several parts of the United States. The United Fruit Company purchased large amounts of land in Central America, and built banana plantations. They invested in more refrigerated ships, as well as large storing and packing facilities to meet the growing demand for bananas. Entire towns in Central America were built around producing bananas for the United Fruit Company. The company built stores, hospitals, schools, and telegraph and telephone lines in the towns. Soon, the United Fruit Company had grown so large that it had swallowed, or taken over, all of the small, local banana growers in Central America.

Competition

In 1899, Joseph, Felix, and Luca Vaccaro, and their business partner Salvador D'Antoni began importing bananas to New Orleans. At first, they were not considered a threat to the United Fruit Company's success, because the Vaccaro brothers' business was so small. The brothers built business relationships with Italian fruit growers in Honduras. By 1906, the Vaccaros controlled ten miles (16 kilometers) of railroad in Honduras, which they used to transport and sell bananas and other tropical fruit within the country. The small business expanded over time, and became known as Standard Fruit in 1968. Standard Fruit became a major competitor to the United Fruit Company.

People in Central America were hired by American-owned fruit companies to work on plantations.

Workers in Honduras load a cargo ship with bananas. In 1910, the United Fruit Company helped overthrow the Honduran government, which had failed to give the company tax breaks.

The Workforce

Both the United Fruit Company and Standard Fruit employed people from Central America to work on their banana plantations. They also hired laborers from India who had **migrated** to Central America to work on the Panama Canal, a man-made waterway across the Isthmus of Panama that now connects the Atlantic and Pacific oceans. Once the canal was finished, most of the workers were hired by the major fruit companies. Often, the workers were paid little for their work on the plantations.

"El Pulpo"

Both the United Fruit Company and Standard Fruit came to control many aspects of the workers' lives. Workers nicknamed the United Fruit Company "El Pulpo," or The Octopus.

It was called the Octopus because the company held power over the workers in many different ways, like the arms of an octopus. Governments in Central and South America wanted the fruit companies to stay, because they created jobs for the people. Fruit companies received **tax breaks** and other benefits from the governments, including large areas of land on which to set up more banana plantations. The fruit companies made a lot of profit, but a very small amount of the money stayed within the countries where bananas were grown. Workers were paid low wages and most of their money went back to the fruit companies who owned stores, schools, and hospitals for workers. Plantation stores were stocked with items that were imported from the United States, rather than from local producers.

Bananas Go to War

From 1914 to 1918, World War I was fought in Europe. Trade between countries almost stopped because of the fighting. The United Fruit Company contributed 37 of its ships to the war effort, which meant that they could no longer export bananas in large quantities. When the war finally ended, the **Great Depression** struck. There were far fewer resources and basic supplies than there had been before the war. Bananas became a luxury item and the major banana companies lost demand for their fruit. The United Fruit Company fired many of its Central American workers. The company also cut the price that they paid independent banana growers for their fruit. Then, after **World War II**, the economies of North America boomed. Many industries and businesses prospered, including the banana trade. Hundreds of acres of jungle were cleared in South and Central America, and the Caribbean, to grow more bananas.

Large amounts of tropical fruit, including bananas, are loaded on a ship in Ecuador to be sent to North America.

Banana Tourism

After World War II, banana companies began building hotels on banana-producing islands in the Caribbean, such as Jamaica. Company ships, including the United Fruit Company's Great White Fleet were furnished with comfortable passenger cabins. The companies began advertising Caribbean cruises to North Americans who, after the war, had money to spend on vacations. The ships were equipped to carry banana shipments, as well as wealthy passengers, between the tropics and North America.

Banana Boom

Refrigerated trucks were developed in the 1940s. The trucks were first **insulated** with grass and sawdust, and were kept cool with barrels of water and ice. The construction of multi-lane highways around this time made it possible to transport bananas to regions further inland, rather than deliver the fruit to ports along the coast. Over time, the trucks became more modernized, and by 1970, banana companies favored them over the refrigerated rail cars and ships that had once brought bananas to North America. At around the same time, several major fruit companies, including United Fruit, joined to form one large **corporation** called United Brands. The company is now known as Chiquita Brands International. Standard Fruit was later purchased by the Dole Corporation.

236   A FLORIDA PEACH IN A BANANA GROVE

A postcard from the 1920s showing a young woman in a banana field. Few bananas are grown in the United States. Most are imported from Central America.

(below) A Chiquita Brands transport truck loaded with bananas prepares to leave Costa Rica.

From Field to Supermarket

Banana plantations are owned by large fruit companies that control growing, harvesting, packing, shipping, and distribution of the fruit to supermarkets. Many of these large-scale banana-growing operations are located in Central America. Banana plantations require huge amounts of land, sometimes up to 5,000 hectares (12,355 acres).

Taking Care of the Fields

Banana plants are sprayed with pesticides and fertilizers so that they stay healthy while they grow. Workers tie the plants to poles so that the plants do not bend when the fruit is mature. It is very important that banana farms are kept free of weeds, because weeds steal nutrients from the soil that the banana plants need to grow. On some farms, geese are allowed to roam between the plants, because they eat the weeds. Another method of getting rid of weeds is to spread a layer of dried banana leaves over the soil.

A banana worker on a plantation in Ecuador covers bananas in plastic bags to protect the fruit from pests.

Harvested bananas are attached to cables that take the fruit from the field to the packing shed.

Working the Fields

Machines are used to clear the land for banana plantations. Workers plant and tend the banana plants by hand. At harvest time, a worker called a cutter cuts down the plant with a machete. Another worker, called a backer, catches the plant as it falls. The plant falls onto a large cushion that is placed on the backer's shoulder. The cushion is to prevent the fruit from bruising when the bananas fall. The cutter then cuts down most of the suckers, but leaves the two largest ones, the daughter and granddaughter, to develop into new banana plants. The backer attaches the fruit to one of the overhead cables that run between the rows of plants. The moving cables bring the bananas to the packing shed.

▲ *Bananas are harvested year-round.*

At the Packing Shed

The packing shed, or processing plant, is located on the banana plantation. At the packing shed, workers remove the bananas from the stem by hand, and separate the fruit into smaller clusters of four to six bananas. The bananas are washed in large tanks full of cold water. The water removes most of the chemicals from the fruit, and also lowers the temperature of the bananas, which are still warm from the field. Inspectors then examine the bananas to make sure that they are of a high enough quality to export. Bananas with cracked, spotted, or bruised skins are not suitable for export. Once the bananas pass inspection, they are packed very carefully into boxes so they will not bump against each other and arrive at their destination bruised.

Putting the Bananas to Sleep

Boxes of bananas are loaded onto huge refrigerated ships, or reefers. Large banana companies, such as Dole and Del Monte, own the ships that transport the fruit to their final destination. The ships are cold enough to prevent the bananas from ripening any further. This stage is called "putting the bananas to sleep." At their destination, reefers dock at food terminals, where they are inspected for insects, snakes, and other tropical pests.

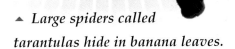

▲ *Large spiders called tarantulas hide in banana leaves.*

Ripening Rooms

After bananas pass inspection, they are brought to special ripening rooms for three to eight days. Ripening rooms are warmer than the reefers and cause the bananas to ripen more before they are brought to supermarkets. Ethylene gas, a substance produced naturally by all fruit, is pumped through the rooms to speed up the ripening process. The temperature of the ripening rooms is lowered as days pass, to stop the bananas from ripening too much before they are loaded onto refrigerated trucks and brought to supermarkets for sale.

Bananas are unloaded from trucks and sold at markets and grocery stores.

Endangered Bananas

Bananas are delicate plants that are sensitive to diseases, pests, and poor weather. Without proper care and constant attention, banana crops fail, resulting in loss of income, and loss of an important food staple.

Weather

Floods can destroy banana crops, tearing the plants out of the ground and pulling out the stakes that keep the plants from falling over. Heavy storms such as hurricanes and tornadoes leave the plants fruitless or rip off the protective leaves. Major windstorms called "blowdowns" can ruin an entire crop in just a few minutes. Blowdowns cause farmers to lose their source of income and often destroy their houses, leaving them and their families homeless.

Black Sigatoka

Black Sigatoka is a fungus that affects nearly all banana-growing regions of the world. The disease first appeared in 1969 in Honduras, quickly spread through South and Central America, and eventually spread to islands in the South Pacific. Black Sigatoka is highly contagious and is easily spread to other plants by the wind. Fungicides help control attacks of Black Sigatoka, but the chemicals are extremely expensive and they are poisonous to the workers who have to handle them.

A Chiquita Brands International plantation destroyed by a hurricane in Honduras. Workers are often the most severely affected because there is no work for them.

Moko Disease

Moko disease is caused by small organisms called bacteria, which infect banana plants and cause them to rot from the inside out. Moko disease is common on banana plantations in the Caribbean, and South and Central America. Insects carrying the disease infect banana plants by burrowing through the fruit. Farm tools, such as machetes, can also spread the disease if there are any of the bacteria on the knife blades. Roots of infected banana plants can infect other banana plants just by touching them. The bacteria cannot be seen, so it is often too late to save crops once Moko disease appears in the plants. Workers help reduce the spread of Moko disease by disinfecting all farm equipment, as well as injecting infected plants with a strong **herbicide**.

Nematodes

Nematodes are worms that usually attack the roots of banana plants. The worms burrow into the root of the banana plants and cause the leaves to turn red, purple, or black. Chemical sprays called nematicides can prevent the worms from attacking the plants. Another way of dealing with nematodes is to tear down the plants and plow the field. Sun eventually kills nematodes, so fields are left unprotected to get rid of the worms. It can take as long as three years before the sun kills all of the nematodes in some fields. Most banana workers cannot live without a source of income for this long, so they choose to deal with nematodes by using chemicals.

The black marks on this banana leaf are from nematodes, tiny worms that destroy banana crops.

Bananas and the Environment

Large banana plantations have left giant holes in tropical rainforests. Huge areas of jungle are cleared to make room to grow the plants. The tropical rainforests are home to thousands of species of plants and animals, some of which are just being discovered by scientists. Wiping out the rainforests means that these species lose their homes, and come one step closer to extinction.

Monoculture

Growing one crop over and over in one area of land is known as monoculture. Monoculture strains the environment by creating an artificial ecosystem. An ecosystem is an environment in which plants and animals live. In monoculture, farmers allow one species to thrive, while killing off many of the other species that would normally live in that particular environment.

Loss of Soil

Farming one crop on the same area of land year after year is harmful to the soil. Land needs time to regenerate, or build up a new supply of nutrients. New land is cleared and farmed until it too becomes barren. While the soil is left bare, it can easily erode, or be blown away by wind or washed away by rains, because there are no plant roots to anchor the soil to the ground. Soil erosion can cause the soil to become too weak to support food crops at all.

A plane sprays chemicals on a banana plantation to keep the banana plants healthy.

Poisonous Pesticides

Many of the pesticides and chemical fertilizers used on banana plantations are toxic, or poisonous, and increase the risk of cancer in the workers. The chemicals are also damaging to the environment. Wind blows the chemicals off of the leaves of banana plants, creating air pollution. The chemicals are also washed into nearby lakes and streams during heaving rainstorms, contaminating, or polluting, the water that banana workers and their families drink. About 40 percent of the chemicals used in banana farming ends up back in the soil, where new plants are grown.

Banana workers from a plantation in Nicaragua protest the use of chemicals on plantations owned by large fruit companies. The workers say that the chemicals are making them ill.

Chemical-Free

Organic bananas are bananas grown without the use of pesticides and other chemicals. Some farmers have begun using coffee husks, fish bones, and seaweed mixed with animal dung to fertilize their fields instead of chemicals. Organic bananas are becoming more popular, but they still account for only a small amount of bananas produced in the world each year. Another way to keep nutrients in the soil is to plant a different crop in between the rows of banana plants. This is called a cover crop. Cover crops prevent the soil from becoming exhausted which can happen when the same crop is grown on the land over and over again. Cover crops, such as grass and soybeans, also help prevent soil erosion.

The Future

Scientists in laboratories try to find new ways of making banana plants resistant to diseases.

Scientists from 11 different countries are involved in a research project to understand the genetic make-up of the dessert banana. The researchers want to introduce new genes to the banana, without changing its flavor, color, and texture. By adding a little genetic variation to the banana, scientists hope that the dessert banana will be able to fight off diseases. This might prevent the dessert banana from going extinct. This will also allow scientists to develop new fertilizers and pesticides that do a better job of fighting diseases and pests. It is hoped that new chemicals would not have to be used as much as the ones that banana farmers use today. This means that workers would not be exposed to such large amounts of chemicals.

A Helping Hand

Many **nonprofit** organizations around the world try to improve the lives of banana workers. The organizations help by raising awareness of working conditions on banana plantations. The organizations also try to convince consumers to boycott companies who do not pay their workers fairly, provide health benefits, or allow the workers to form **unions**. Land use is another problem that concerns consumers. Most of the bananas that are grown without the help of chemicals are still grown on areas that were once rainforest. Many organizations encourage consumers to buy locally grown produce, rather than produce grown by large transnational corporations.

Fair Trade Bananas

Fair trade is a term that describes farmers receiving a fair, or decent, price for their products. Fair trade bananas are more expensive to buy at the market, but farmers receive a greater share of the profits, because the fruit are not delivered or grown by large fruit companies. To be a fair trade farm, banana farmers must reduce their chemical use and make an effort to use natural fertilizers. Farmers who register as a fair trade farm are guaranteed a minimum price for their bananas, and are also given an additional sum of money to help cover their production costs. Farmers are also given money with which they are encouraged to improve working conditions for their employees.

At this school in Dominica, a Caribbean country, students received new desks thanks to a fair trade organization.

Glossary

Arab traders People from what is now Saudi Arabia, who in the past were known as great traders

Christianity A religion that believes in one god and follows the teachings of Jesus Christ

colonist A settler who comes from a ruling land with the intent of staying

commercial Intended for sale or profit

consume To eat, drink, or in some way use up

corporation A large business

cultivate To farm and harvest a crop

edible Able to be eaten

export To sell to another country

extinct No longer in existence

fertile Able to produce

fungicides Chemicals used to destroy fungi

Great Depression A period during the 1930s of high unemployment and a weak economy

herbicide A chemical that kills plants

insulate To add or cover with a material that helps to maintain a temperature

migrate To move from one country to another

missionaries People who go to another land to teach others about their religion

monopoly Having sole control over a certain commodity, or good

New World The name Europeans gave to North, South, and Central America

nonprofit Not intended to make a profit

oversee To watch or guard over

pandemic Something, such as a disease, that spreads over large areas

pesticides Chemicals used to kill pests

pithy Stem-like

reproduction Producing the next generation

shoot New growth

staple A main or essential part

tax break Having to pay less tax, or money to the government

tropics The warm areas of the world located just north and south of the equator

union An organization that fights for the rights of workers for such things as better pay

variety A type

vegetative propagation The ability of some plants to reproduce without male and female parts

volcanic ash Tiny pieces of rock from a volcanic eruption

vulnerable At risk of being hurt

World War II An international war in Europe and Asia that took place from 1939 to 1945

Index

1 2 3 4 5 6 7 8 9 0 Printed in the U.S.A. 4 3 2 1 0 9 8 7 6 5